own your worth

A 30-Day Devotional for Anyone Who's Ever Felt Not Enough

The Anchored Devotional Series
Book Two

emery knox

Copyright © 2025 by RMC Publishers

All rights reserved.

No part of this publication may be reproduced in any form, or by any means, electronic or mechanical, including photocopying, recording, or any information browsing, storage, or retrieval system, without prior permission in writing from the publisher.

Under no circumstance will any blame or legal responsibility be held against the publisher, or author, for any damages, reparation, or monetary loss due to the information contained within this book. Either directly or indirectly. You are responsible for your own choices, actions, and results.

Please note the information contained within this document is for educational and entertainment purposes only. All e!ort has been executed to present accurate, up-to-date, and reliable, complete information. No warranties of any kind are declared or implied. Readers acknowledge that the author is not engaging in the rendering of legal, financial, medical, or professional advice. The content within this book has been derived from various sources. Please consult a licensed professional before attempting any techniques outlined in this book.

www.rmcpublishers.com

contents

Introduction	v
Day 1: You Are Already Enough	1
Day 2: You're Not a Mistake	5
Day 3: Stop Shrinking to Fit	9
Day 4: Stop Chasing Gold Stars	13
Day 5: Made for the Deep End	17
Day 6: Not a Project to Fix	21
Day 7: You Don't Have to Earn It	25
Day 8: You're Already Chosen	29
Day 9: Take Up Space	33
Day 10: Grace Doesn't Keep Score	37
Day 11: Speak Kindly to Yourself	41
Day 12: You Are More Than What You Do	45
Day 13: Stop Apologizing for Existing	49
Day 14: You're Not Falling Behind	53
Day 15: Be Gentle With Yourself	57
Day 16: You Are Not a Burden	61
Day 17: Loved Before You Did Anything	65
Day 18: Your Pace Has Purpose	69
Day 19: Your Story Isn't Small	73
Day 20: You Are Not Too Late	77
Day 21: You Don't Need to Earn Love	81
Day 22: Your Voice Matters	85
Day 23: Trust the Unfolding	89
Day 24: Live from Your Worth	93
Day 25: You're Allowed to Be a Work in Progress	97
Day 26: You Were Never Too Much	101
Day 27: Stay Soft	105
Day 28: You Are Allowed to Take Up Joy	109

Day 29: You're More Than Your Low Moments	113
Day 30: The Work Was Worth It	117
Conclusion: Keep Showing Up	121
Before You Go…	123

introduction

Hey,

Let's pause for a second. Before you flip to Day 1, before the Scripture and the journaling and the songs. Just take a breath. In and out.

Now ask yourself: *Have I ever felt like I wasn't enough?*

Not smart enough. Not pretty enough. Not spiritual enough. Not productive, popular, lovable, or worthy enough.

If you said yes, this book is for you.

And if you said no? Maybe read it twice.

You're holding a 30-day devotional written for the moments when self-worth feels like a moving target. For the days when comparison crushes you, when impostor syndrome screams louder than truth, when you don't feel worthy of love, success, or grace. It's for the nights you scroll through your feed and wonder why everyone else seems to have it figured out—why you still feel like a question mark.

But here's what I hope you remember:

You don't have to hustle to be worthy.

You don't have to shrink to be loved.

Introduction

You don't have to earn your value.

You already have it.

This book isn't about fixing you, it's about reminding you of what's always been true: You are deeply known, chosen, and loved, not despite your mess, but in the middle of it.

You'll find 30 short, soul-honest reflections, one for each day plus journal questions, breath prayers, and connection with music and art. You'll explore Scripture not as a checklist, but as a conversation. You'll breathe. You'll reflect. You'll remember your worth.

Here's how it works:

- Every day includes one Scripture (we keep it real)
- A reflection (raw and relevant)
- 3 journaling questions (no wrong answers)
- A bold quote to remember
- An affirmation or breath prayer to ground you
- A song that feels like a hug
- One creative anchor (image, art, or story)
- And a tiny action step to help you live what you've read

Don't worry about being perfect. Skip a day? Come back. Cry? Let it be holy. Doubt? Bring it. You don't have to clean up to come close to God. This is about getting honest, not getting it "right."

So if you've ever whispered, *I don't think I'm enough,*

this book was written to whisper back:

You are. You really, really are.

Let's begin.

—Emery

day 1: you are already enough

Scripture

"I praise you because I am fearfully and wonderfully made; your works are wonderful, I know that full well." — Psalm 139:14 (NIV)

Reflection

Let's start with the thing most people never say out loud: *Sometimes I don't like who I am.* Not just on a bad hair day or when your jeans don't fit right, but deeper. On the inside. The part of you that worries you're too much or not enough. The part that tries hard and still feels like a disappointment.

But here's something radical: *You are already enough.*

Not when you lose the weight. Not when you hit your goals. Not when you get over that thing you don't talk about. Now. As you are.

Psalm 139 says you're fearfully and wonderfully made—not *potentially*, not *after you get your act together*—now. God didn't mess up when He made you. He didn't roll the dice. You weren't stitched together by accident. You were designed with intention. Not perfect, but purposeful.

The world will try to convince you otherwise. That your worth is something you earn, prove, or polish. That you have to be louder,

Own Your Worth

quieter, cuter, calmer, more productive, more spiritual, more whatever. But here's the truth: worth doesn't come from comparison. It comes from the One who created you.

You don't have to chase it. You get to claim it.

So let this be the first step: not striving to become worthy, but *starting* with the belief that you already are. Because you are. God said so.

Journaling Questions

• When was the first time you remember feeling "not enough"? What made you feel that way?

• What would change in your life if you believed you were already enough, without doing anything extra?

• How do you think God sees you compared to how you see yourself?

Real Talk Quote

You don't become enough, you remember that you already are.

Breath Prayer

Inhale: I am made on purpose.

Exhale: I am already enough.

Day 1: You Are Already Enough

Need a soundtrack for today's reflection?

Scan to listen to "Mirror" by Madison Ryann Ward.

This soulful, emotionally resonant track is all about reflection, identity, and learning to see yourself clearly. A perfect match for a Day 1 theme about reclaiming self-worth and embracing the truth of who you are.

Creative Anchor

In a small town, a baker was known for her perfectly imperfect loaves. The crust was always a little uneven, and the shape was never quite symmetrical. But every Saturday, people lined up down the block. When asked why her bread was so popular, she said, "Because I use my hands, not machines. You can taste the love in every lump and curve."

You are like that bread, not factory-made or mass-produced, but lovingly hand-shaped by a Creator who didn't aim for uniformity. The so-called "flaws" in you? They're fingerprints of intention. You're not here to be polished into sameness, you're here to be real. Fully human. Fully loved. Fully enough.

Try This

Take ten minutes today and write a letter to yourself that begins: "Here's what I love about you…"

No editing. No judgment. Just let it flow. You don't need to share it with anyone. Let it be a mirror, not of what you think you *should* be, but of who you already are.

day 2: you're not a mistake

Scripture

"For we are God's masterpiece. He has created us anew in Christ Jesus, so we can do the good things he planned for us long ago." — Ephesians 2:10 (NLT)

Reflection

There's a quiet lie that seeps in sometimes, the one that says you're a cosmic accident, a filler character in someone else's story. But Ephesians shouts over that whisper with something truer, louder, and more lasting: *You are God's masterpiece.*

Not a mess-up. Not a mistake. A masterpiece.

That means you were created with intention. With beauty. With purpose woven into your very existence. God didn't just *happen* to make you — He crafted you, uniquely and deliberately, to carry out good things in this world that only you can do.

Even when life feels like a series of wrong turns, you're still walking the path of someone beloved. Even when your confidence crumbles, your Creator's care does not.

And those "good things"? They aren't flashy titles or perfect performances. Sometimes they look like kindness to a friend, courage to keep going, or simply showing up when it's hard.

Own Your Worth

So the next time that old story surfaces, the one that says you don't matter , come back to this truth:

You are a masterpiece.

You are made new.

And you have a purpose no one else can fulfill.

Journaling Questions

- What moments or messages have made you question your worth?
- How does it feel to imagine God designed you with love and intention?
- What truth can you hold onto when you feel "not enough"?

Real Talk Quote

You are not a mistake to fix. You're a masterpiece in progress.

Breath Prayer

Inhale: I am made with care.

Exhale: I am wonderfully made.

Day 2: You're Not a Mistake

Need a soundtrack for today's reflection?

Scan to listen to "Who I Am" by Wyn Starks.

A powerful anthem about showing up fully, unapclogetically, and beautifully in your own skin.

Creative Anchor

Even unfinished art is still art. You are being shaped, not broken.

Try This

Write down three things about yourself that you believe God sees and delights in, even if you're still learning to believe them yourself. Tape them to your mirror.

day 3: stop shrinking to fit

Scripture

"Am I now trying to win the approval of human beings, or of God? Or am I trying to please people? If I were still trying to please people, I would not be a servant of Christ."

— Galatians 1:10 (NIV)

Reflection

You've probably done it without realizing. Dimmed your excitement so you wouldn't come off "too much." Edited your captions to sound cooler. Stayed silent when you wanted to speak up. All to fit in. All to be liked. All to not take up too much space.

It's exhausting.

And somewhere along the line, shrinking feels like survival, like the only way to stay connected, accepted, safe. But what if you weren't made to shrink? What if your fullness isn't a problem to solve, but a gift to offer?

Galatians 1:10 is a reminder: living for the approval of others is a trap. You'll never feel enough if your worth is always up for a vote. But the moment you stop contorting yourself to meet everyone else's expectations, that's where freedom begins. That's where your God-given worth starts to rise up.

Own Your Worth

You weren't called to be palatable. You were called to be powerful. You weren't created to perform. You were created to reflect the image of a wildly creative, loving God and there's nothing small or quiet about that.

So today, notice the moments you feel the urge to shrink. And gently remind yourself: You don't need to fit in to belong. You already do.

Journaling Questions

- When have you felt the need to shrink or hide parts of yourself to be accepted?
- What parts of you feel "too much" and what would it look like to embrace them?
- How can you remind yourself today that you already belong?

Real Talk Quote

Stop shrinking. The world needs the real you, not the filtered one.

Breath Prayer

Inhale: I am not too much

Exhale: I am enough

Day 3: Stop Shrinking to Fit

Need a soundtrack for today's reflection?

Scan to listen to "Flowers" by Miley Cyrus.

This self-empowerment anthem reminds you that you don't need to seek validation outside yourself to feel whole.

Creative Anchor

You were never meant to fit into their box.

Try This

Write down one thing you've been holding back out of fear of being "too much." Say it out loud today, even just to yourself. Let it live in the light.

day 4: stop chasing gold stars

Scripture

"Cease striving and know that I am God." — Psalm 46:10 (NASB)

Reflection

Ever feel like you're performing all the time? Like your worth depends on how well you show up, speak up, keep it together, or impress the people around you?

That's not freedom, that's survival mode. And it's exhausting.

The truth is: you don't have to prove your worth by being impressive, liked, productive, or pleasing. You don't need the applause of strangers or the validation of people who don't even know the full you. You need truth, the kind that doesn't shift with opinions or fade when you're not at your best.

God never asked you to prove anything. He already called you chosen, known, and enough.

When you live from that place, the pressure drops. You can stop hustling for love and start resting in it. You can show up honestly, even when you're struggling. You don't have to wear a mask.

So today, let go of the need to perform. You don't need to prove your worth — you just need to remember it..

Own Your Worth

Journaling Questions

- Where in your life do you feel like you're constantly "performing" or seeking approval?
- What would change if you believed God already approved of you, fully, right now?
- How can you practice showing up without the pressure to impress?

Real Talk Quote

You don't need a spotlight to be seen by God.

Breath Prayer / Affirmation

Inhale: I am already seen.

Exhale: I don't have to prove anything.

Need a soundtrack for today's reflection?

Scan to listen to "Steady Heart" by Steffany Gretzinger.

A gentle reminder that even when life is uncertain, God remains unshakably steady.

Day 4: Stop Chasing Gold Stars

Creative Anchor

Remember being a kid and lining up at school, hoping for a gold star on your worksheet? That tiny sticker felt like proof you mattered — that you were doing something right. Now the stars just look different: likes, grades, compliments, hustle points. But the ache is the same.

God isn't keeping a sticker chart. He's not waiting at the end of your productivity for permission to love you. His approval isn't performance-based, it's presence-based. He delights in you before you do a thing.

So exhale. You're not in a race. You're already seen, already valued. The gold stars don't make you worthy, they've just distracted you from the truth that you always were.

Try This

Take ten slow breaths with one hand on your chest and the other on your stomach. As you breathe, whisper, "I am loved. I can be still." Let your body memorize the feeling of being accepted without earning it.

day 5: made for the deep end

Scripture

"The Spirit you received does not make you slaves, so that you live in fear again; rather, the Spirit you received brought about your adoption to sonship." — Romans 8:15 (NIV)

Reflection

You weren't made for the shallow life, the surface-level conversations, the fake smiles, the pretending that everything's fine when it's not. You were made for the deep end.

For realness. For big feelings. For wild faith. For soul-level belonging.

But sometimes, being someone who feels deeply in a world that often stays on the surface can make you question your worth. You might wonder, *Why do I care so much? Why can't I just chill?* The answer: because you're wired for more.

You've got a heart tuned to depth, meaning, and love that doesn't play games. That's not weakness, that's your strength. That's the Spirit inside you reminding you that you were adopted into something real and fierce and freeing. You don't have to perform for love. You don't have to blend in to be accepted.

You've been chosen. Fully. Completely. No masks required.

Own Your Worth

So if you ever feel like you're too heavy, too intense, too real—remember: you're not made for the shallow end. You're made for waters where your soul can stretch and breathe.

Journaling Questions

- What parts of your personality feel "too deep" for others, but true to you?
- Where in your life are you still trying to stay in the shallow end to feel safe?
- What would it look like to live like you've already been chosen?

Real Talk Quote

You weren't made to tread water—you were made to dive deep.

Breath Prayer

Inhale: I am chosen.

Exhale: I don't have to perform.

Need a soundtrack for today's reflection?

Scan to listen to "Deep Water" by American Authors.

Day 5: Made for the Deep End

Creative Anchor

The deep is where I come alive.

Prompt: Imagine yourself in deep water—safe, weightless, held.

day 6: not a project to fix

Scripture

"The Lord your God is with you, the Mighty Warrior who saves. He will take great delight in you; in his love he will no longer rebuke you, but will rejoice over you with singing." — Zephaniah 3:17 (NIV)

Reflection

Sometimes we treat ourselves like unfinished business.

We obsess over what's wrong, what's missing, what still needs fixing. We zoom in on every flaw, every failure, every part of us that doesn't feel "there" yet.

But what if you're not a project?

What if you're a person—a *whole* person—already worthy of love and belonging, even while you're still growing?

God didn't create you with a label that says "under construction." You're not some abandoned building waiting to be made presentable. You are *fearfully and wonderfully made*. That means right now, with the stretch marks and the self-doubt and the dreams you're still chasing—you're a masterpiece. Not someday. Not after you get it together. Now.

This doesn't mean there's no room for healing or growth. But the *starting point* matters. You don't start broken. You start beloved.

Own Your Worth

So when the inner critic turns up the volume, telling you you're too messy, too late, too much, remind yourself: *I'm not a problem to solve. I'm a wonder to be witnessed.*

That shift? It might just change everything.

Journaling Questions

- What parts of yourself have you been trying to "fix" instead of accepting?
- How might your life feel different if you believed you are already enough?
- What would self-worth look like without conditions?

Real Talk Quote

You're not a project to fix—you're a wonder in progress.

Breath Prayer

Inhale: I begin with love.

Exhale: I don't need to prove my worth.

Day 6: Not a Project to Fix

Need a soundtrack for today's reflection?

Scan to listen to "Little Voice" by Sara Bareilles.

This song beautifully captures the struggle of self-doubt and the courage to listen to one's inner voice. It's gentle and empowering and resonates with the feeling of finally believing in one's worth.

Creative Anchor

Story: Imagine walking into an art gallery and seeing a massive, unfinished painting. Someone whispers, "It's not done," but the artist, standing nearby, smiles and says, "It is exactly how I meant it to be."

Even in progress, you are already art.

day 7: you don't have to earn it

Scripture

"This is love: not that we loved God, but that he loved us and sent his Son as an atoning sacrifice for our sins." — 1 John 4:10 (NIV)

Reflection

We live in a world that rewards hustle.

Work harder, be better, do more and maybe, just maybe, you'll be enough.

So it makes sense that sometimes we treat God's love the same way.

If I just prayed more, helped more, sinned less… *then* I'd be worthy, right?

But here's the wild truth:

You never had to earn God's love.

He didn't wait for you to be "good enough" before stepping in. He loved you first, before the glow-up, before the apology, before the belief even kicked in.

That kind of love doesn't make sense by human standards. It's unfair in the best way.

Own Your Worth

This means your highlight reel, grades, likes, or spiritual record don't measure your worth.

It means you don't have to fake it. You can breathe.

Letting that truth sink in that you are already loved, already chosen changes how you walk through the world. Not from a place of striving, but from a place of security. You begin to serve from joy, not pressure. To show up because you want to, not because you're afraid not to.

You don't have to earn what's already yours.

Love came looking for you first.

Journaling Questions

• How have you tried to "earn" love or approval?

• How does it feel to be reminded that God loved you first?

• What could change in your life if you stopped striving to be worthy?

Real Talk Quote

You don't have to hustle for what heaven already gave you.

Breath Prayer

Inhale: I am already loved.

Exhale: I don't have to prove it.

Day 7: You Don't Have to Earn It

Need a soundtrack for today's reflection?

Scan to listen to "Touch the Sky" by Hillsong UNITED.

Creative Anchor

When love is a gift, all you have to do is receive it.

day 8: you're already chosen

Scripture

"But you are a chosen people, a royal priesthood, a holy nation, God's special possession, that you may declare the praises of him who called you out of darkness into his wonderful light." — 1 Peter 2:9 (NIV)

Reflection

There's something wild about being picked. Whether it's getting a text first, being offered the job, or someone saying, "I see you — and I want *you*," it hits deep. It's one thing to be liked. Another thing to be loved. But to be *chosen*? That's next level.

We spend so much energy trying to prove ourselves. To show we're worth the invite, the spot, the role. But here's the thing: God didn't wait for your résumé. He chose you long before you felt worthy. Long before you believed you had something to offer. Long before you even knew you needed to be chosen.

You are not a backup plan. Not a second choice. Not a "maybe someday." You are God's "yes." You were seen in full and still picked — flaws, doubts, and all. You don't have to perform, shrink, or hustle to be enough. You already are. The choosing has already happened.

So when the world makes you feel like you must beg for attention, approval, or space, remember this: you've already been named, claimed, and called. No vote. No audition. Just grace.

Journaling Questions

- What areas of your life feel like you're waiting to be "picked"?
- How does knowing you're already chosen by God change how you see yourself?
- What would it look like to live like you're already enough, already loved?

Real Talk Quote

You don't have to earn the spotlight, you were made to shine in it.

Breath Prayer

Inhale: I am already chosen

Exhale: I am already loved

Day 8: You're Already Chosen

Need a soundtrack for today's reflection?

Listen to "Golden Hour" by JVKE.

A mainstream track full of beauty, awe, and being seen; a modern metaphor for being chosen in an unexpected moment.

Creative Anchor

Micro-Scene

Imagine being handed a key with your name engraved on it. No test, no questions. Just yours. That's belonging.

Try This

Write a sticky note that says "Chosen. Loved. Enough." and place it where you'll see it every morning.

day 9: take up space

Scripture

"The boundary lines have fallen for me in pleasant places; surely I have a delightful inheritance." — Psalm 16:6 (NIV)

Reflection

You don't need permission to exist.

To speak.

To show up in full color.

To take up space.

Somewhere along the way, many of us were taught to shrink. To tone it down. To be more polite, more quiet, more palatable. Maybe you were told your ideas were "too much" or your dreams were too unrealistic. Perhaps you learned to apologize for everything even things that weren't your fault. Maybe you began to see your presence as a burden instead of a gift.

But hear this: You were never meant to live in the margins.

God crafted your soul with intention. He didn't make you vibrant and bold just to have you dim your light. The boundary lines of your life — your body, your voice, your identity are sacred. You're

Own Your Worth

allowed to define them. You're allowed to honor them. You're allowed to walk with your head held high.

Taking up space isn't arrogance, it's stewardship. It's saying, "I will no longer apologize for existing." You were created with purpose. You belong in every room God opens for you. Your worth is not up for negotiation.

So today, breathe deeply, unclench your shoulders, speak a little louder, and laugh a little freer. You have full permission to take up space.

Journaling Questions

- Where in your life have you felt the need to shrink or apologize?
- What's one way you can physically or emotionally take up more space today?
- How does Psalm 16:6 speak to your sense of belonging?

Real Talk Quote

You were never too much, just in the wrong room.

Breath Prayer

Inhale: I am allowed to be here.

Exhale: I will not shrink myself.

Day 9: Take Up Space

Need a soundtrack for today's reflection?

Scan to listen to "Confident" by Demi Lovato.

Creative Anchor

You were made for spacious places.

Try This

Stand tall in front of a mirror. Take up physical space. Practice saying a boundary out loud, even if it's just for you.

day 10: grace doesn't keep score

Scripture

"The faithful love of the Lord never ends! His mercies never cease. Great is his faithfulness; his mercies begin afresh each morning." — Lamentations 3:22–23 (NLT)

Reflection

There's this exhausting idea out there that you've got to *deserve* love. Earn your spot. Hustle for grace. Be good enough, spiritual enough, healed enough. But grace isn't something that responds to performance. It exists *because* we fall short.

Think about it: if love had to be earned, we'd all be in trouble. Every stumble, every mess, every bad day would disqualify us. But that's not how it works in the kingdom of God. Grace shows up **before** you get it together. It walks in when you think you've lost your way, when your hands are empty, and your heart is tired.

If you grew up believing you had to prove your worth — to God, to people, even to yourself — then here's your permission slip: You don't have to keep score. God's not asking you to measure up. He already sees you, already knows you, and already loves you. Fully.

You were never meant to live in a courtroom of your own making. So, call off the trial. Drop the evidence. Grace has already declared you enough.

Own Your Worth

Journaling Questions
- What are some ways you've tried to "earn" love or acceptance?
- What would change if you fully received God's grace, no strings attached?
- Who in your life needs grace from me today?

Real Talk Quote

You don't have to hustle for grace. It has already found you.

Breath Prayer

Inhale: I am not earning love.

Exhale: I am already enough.

Need a soundtrack for today's reflection?

Scan to listen to "Beloved" by Jordan Feliz.

Day 10: Grace Doesn't Keep Score

Creative Anchor

You're running late. The day's already off-track, and your to-do list is growing. But then a friend texts: *"Just thinking of you. No need to reply."* No expectations. No demands. Just kindness that doesn't ask you to earn it.

That's grace. It shows up quietly, not because you deserved it, but because love doesn't keep score.

Try This

Send someone a note, a meme, or a prayer, not because they earned it, but because grace is contagious. Then let yourself receive it too.

day 11: speak kindly to yourself

Scripture

"The tongue has the power of life and death, and those who love it will eat its fruit." — Proverbs 18:21 (NIV)

Reflection

Let's be honest. Some of the worst things we hear aren't from other people, they're from our own thoughts. The inner critic? He's loud, relentless, and often ruthless. He tells you you're behind. He mocks your efforts. He plays back mistakes like a broken record. And if we're not careful, we believe every word.

But here's the truth: God never called you by your failures. He never whispered, "You're not enough." That voice in your head? That's fear, insecurity, old wounds, not Him. Scripture reminds us that our words carry life or death. That includes the ones we speak to ourselves in silence.

Would you talk to a friend the way you speak to yourself? Would you roll your eyes at their dreams or critique their every move? Probably not. So why do we treat ourselves with so little grace?

Speaking kindly to yourself isn't self-indulgent, it's spiritual discipline. It's aligning your inner voice with what God already says about you. You are loved. You are capable. You are made on purpose. When your self-talk matches God's truth, things start to shift.

Own Your Worth

So try this: next time that cruel voice shows up, pause. Replace it with something gentler, truer. Talk to yourself like someone worth rooting for — because you are.

Journaling Questions

• What's one lie you regularly tell yourself? What truth can replace it?

• Think of a time you showed yourself grace. How did it feel?

• What phrase could you start repeating to yourself daily?

Real Talk Quote

Talk to yourself like someone who deserves to be loved, because you do.

Breath Prayer

Inhale: I am loved.

Exhale: I will speak like it.

Need a soundtrack for today's reflection?

Scan to listen to "Girl in the Mirror" by Bebe Rexha.

Day 11: Speak Kindly to Yourself

Creative Anchor

Imagine a little kid holding a microphone on a big stage, voice shaking, heart pounding. That kid is you — the younger version still tucked inside. Now imagine walking up beside them, kneeling down, and whispering: "You're doing great. I'm so proud of you. You're safe with me."

That's what it means to speak kindly to yourself, to show up for your inner self with love, not judgment.

Try This

Find a photo of yourself as a child, maybe around 5 or 6 years old. Look at that kid for a moment. Then write a short note of encouragement to them, as if you were their biggest cheerleader. Say the things you wish you'd heard back then. Tape it somewhere visible this week. Let that voice, the kind, gentle one become the loudest.

day 12: you are more than what you do

Scripture

"For we are God's masterpiece. He has created us anew in Christ Jesus, so we can do the good things he planned for us long ago." — Ephesians 2:10 (NLT)

Reflection

You've probably been praised for being productive, driven, or helpful. Like your value comes from how much you can get done or give away. Maybe you're the one who shows up, holds it together, and crosses the finish line even when no one's watching. And maybe, just maybe, you're tired.

The world is loud about "hustle" and "leveling up," but here's something quieter, softer, truer: You are not what you produce. Your worth doesn't begin with your to-do list. It starts with your being — with the simple, sacred fact that you exist and you're loved.

You're more than your resume. More than your GPA. More than your output on a slow day. More than your unread messages, your unpaid internship, your broken routines. You don't have to be impressive to be valuable. You just have to be you.

God doesn't call you a project. He calls you a masterpiece.

Own Your Worth

When you forget that, pause. Breathe. Let yourself remember that you were created in love, not pressure, saved by grace, not performance, and held by someone who never asked you to earn your place.

Journaling Questions

- When do you most feel like your worth is tied to your productivity?
- What part of you needs permission to rest or just be?
- What would it feel like to believe you're enough without doing anything at all?

Real Talk Quote

You are not your hustle. You're already holy.

Breath Prayer

Inhale: I am not what I do.

Exhale: I am loved as I am.

Need a soundtrack for today's reflection?

Scan to listen to "Peace Be Still" by Hope Darst.

Day 12: You Are More Than What You Do

Creative Anchor

You are not your lists or labels,

not your grades or goals.

Not the neatness of your planner,

or how well you play your roles.

You are not your inbox,

your calendar, your pace,

You are something softer, sacred,

held entirely by grace.

You don't have to hustle

for love that's already true.

You are more than what you manage,

You are more than what you do.

Try This

Block off 20 minutes today for something "unproductive" that brings you joy — a nap, a doodle, a walk with no destination. Just be.

day 13: stop apologizing for existing

Scripture

"So now there is no condemnation for those who belong to Christ Jesus."
— Romans 8:1 (NLT)

Reflection

Have you ever noticed how often you say "sorry"?

Sorry for taking up space.

Sorry for asking a question.

Sorry for speaking up or not speaking fast enough.

Sorry for having needs, emotions, or boundaries.

Sometimes "sorry" becomes a reflex when you feel like you're in the way, like your very existence might be too much for someone else to handle. But here's the truth: you were never created to walk around apologizing for being human.

You are not a burden. You are not a bother. You don't need to shrink, smooth things over, or make yourself smaller to be accepted. God doesn't look at you with disappointment — He looks at you with delight. He doesn't roll His eyes when you show up. He rejoices.

Own Your Worth

There's no condemnation here. Not for your past. Not for your mistakes. Not for the weird, messy, still-learning parts of you.

You don't have to earn the right to take up space. You already belong.

Journaling Questions

• What's something you've apologized for that didn't need an apology?

• Where in your life have you felt like "too much" or "not enough"?

• What would change if you believed you didn't have to apologize for existing?

Real Talk Quote

You're not in the way. You're in the room on purpose.

Breath Prayer

Inhale: I am not a mistake.

Exhale: I am welcomed here.

Need a soundtrack for today's reflection?

Scan to listen to "I Got to Live" by Sam Fischer.

Day 13: Stop Apologizing for Existing

Creative Anchor

A tiny poem, tucked like a note in your pocket:

You are not noise.

You are music.

You are not a shadow.

You are light.

You are not in the way.

You are already welcome.

Let it echo in your chest today.

Try This

Start noticing how often you apologize for just existing. Every time the urge to say "sorry" shows up, pause. Ask yourself: *Did I actually do something wrong, or am I just trying to take up less space?*

Then, rewrite the moment.

Instead of "Sorry I'm talking too much," say "Thank you for listening."

Instead of "Sorry for having an opinion," try "I appreciate the space to share."

Take it a step further: write your own "permission slip" today. Just a sentence or two. Something like:

"I have the right to be here, just as I am."

"I don't have to apologize for being human."

"My voice matters."

Stick it to your mirror, tuck it in your journal, or carry it in your wallet. Let it remind you: you never need to shrink to be accepted.

day 14: you're not falling behind

Scripture

"The Lord will guide you always; he will satisfy your needs in a sun-scorched land and will strengthen your frame." — Isaiah 58:11 (NIV)

Reflection

You scroll through your feed and see it: people getting married, graduating, launching businesses, buying houses, publishing highlight reels. And then there's you — still figuring things out, still healing, still waiting for something to click. It can feel like everyone's ahead of you while you're running in place.

But life isn't a checklist. And God's plan for you isn't on a timer.

You are not behind. You are becoming.

There is no single timeline that defines success or purpose. What you perceive as a delay might actually be divine pacing — a slower, deeper path, building something unshakable inside you. God knows the desert seasons, the paused plans, the times you feel forgotten. But Isaiah reminds us: even in sun-scorched places, God will guide, satisfy, and strengthen you.

So take a breath. Don't measure your life by someone else's moments. Measure it by your faithfulness to keep going, to keep growing in grace, even when it's quiet. Slow progress is still sacred.

Own Your Worth

Your journey is unfolding exactly as it should, one honest, intentional step at a time.

You are not late. You are right on time for the life you're meant to live.

Journaling Questions

- Where do you feel like you're "behind" compared to others?
- How can you start trusting God's unique timing for your life?
- What would it look like to honor your current season instead of rushing through it?

Real Talk Quote

Your life is not on pause, it's unfolding at your own perfect pace.

Breath Prayer

Inhale: I am not behind

Exhale: I am exactly where I need to be

Need a soundtrack for today's reflection?

Scan to listen to "This Is Me Now" by Jennifer Lopez.

Day 14: You're Not Falling Behind

Creative Anchor

Beauty is in the becoming.

Try This

Write a kind letter to your younger self. Thank them for not giving up. Reassure them that you're still becoming and it's enough.

day 15: be gentle with yourself

Scripture

"The Lord is compassionate and gracious, slow to anger, abounding in love." — Psalm 103:8 (NIV)

Reflection

You wouldn't talk to a friend the way you sometimes speak to yourself. The sighs. The criticism. The mental tally of all the ways you think you've messed up. The voice in your head that whispers, *You should be better by now.*

But God doesn't speak to you like that. His voice is wrapped in compassion. And maybe it's time yours was, too.

The world moves fast and demands a lot. But your soul doesn't grow through pressure, it grows through grace. You are allowed to be a work in progress. You're allowed to need rest, to get it wrong, to be learning. Self-worth doesn't come from perfection, it comes from knowing that even on your worst days, you are still loved.

When you're trying to grow but feel like you're failing, be gentle. When your mind spirals with comparison, be gentle. When all you can manage is just showing up, that's still enough. Gentleness isn't weakness, it's strength with softness, power with kindness. It's what allows healing to happen.

Own Your Worth

God is not waiting for you to get it together before He shows up with love. He is love, already here, already whispering: *Be kind to yourself. I am.*

Journaling Questions

- What's something you've been hard on yourself about lately?
- How would your inner world change if you spoke to yourself with compassion?
- What's one gentle truth you can hold onto today?

Real Talk Quote

Talk to yourself like someone you're trying to heal, not someone you're trying to fix.

Breath Prayer

Inhale: I am learning

Exhale: I will be gentle with myself

Need a soundtrack for today's reflection?

Scan to listen to "Rainbow" by Kacey Musgraves.

Day 15: Be Gentle With Yourself

Creative Anchor

A girl sits on the bathroom floor, tears running down her face after a long, overwhelming day. She reaches for her phone, not to scroll, not to distract, but to play her favorite calming playlist. Then she runs a warm bath. Lights a candle. Puts on the sweatshirt that feels like safety.

No one told her to. No one's watching. But somewhere deep down, she decided: I'm going to care for myself like I matter.

That's what gentleness looks like. It's not flashy. It's not loud. It's the small decision to choose kindness over criticism, softness over shame, again and again.

Try This

Tonight, treat yourself like someone worth taking care of. Light a candle. Put on your coziest clothes. Do one comforting thing such as a warm bath, your favorite tea, a slow playlist, a journal entry with no pressure to be profound. Let it be an act of gentleness, not indulgence. You just have to allow it.

day 16: you are not a burden

Scripture

"Carry each other's burdens, and in this way you will fulfill the law of Christ." — Galatians 6:2 (NIV)

Reflection

Somewhere along the way, you might have picked up the belief that needing help makes you a burden. Maybe it came from a parent who was emotionally unavailable. Maybe from friends who vanished when things got messy. Or maybe it came from culture — this idea that independence is strength and vulnerability is weakness.

But here's the truth: You are not too much. Your needs are not annoying. Your emotions are not too big. You are not a burden.

God designed us for connection, not just to help others, but to be helped. That's what Galatians 6:2 is all about: carrying *each other's* burdens. There's no shame in needing someone to hold space for you. In fact, asking for help can be one of the most courageous things you do.

When you isolate yourself out of fear of being "too much," you rob people of the chance to love you. And you rob yourself of the experience of being loved exactly as you are.

Own Your Worth

You are not a project to be managed or a weight to be tolerated. You are a person worthy of care, belonging, and tenderness. Your presence is not a problem to solve. It's a gift.

Let people in. Let yourself be seen. You don't have to carry it all alone.

Journaling Questions

- Have you ever believed that your needs made you a burden? Where do you think that belief came from?
- Who in your life makes space for your whole self, and how can you lean into that connection?
- What would it feel like to believe you're not too much?

Real Talk Quote

You're not asking for too much, you're just asking the wrong people.

Breath Prayer

Inhale: I am not a burden

Exhale: I am worthy of love and care

Need a soundtrack for today's reflection?

Scan to listen to "Let Go" by Frou Frou.

Day 16: You Are Not a Burden

Creative Anchor

Picture this: a little kid dragging a backpack twice their size — stuffed with worries, sadness, questions they don't know how to ask. They're wobbling under the weight, not because they packed wrong, but because no one told them it was okay to share the load.

Now imagine someone walking up beside them, kneeling down, and gently lifting part of that bag onto their own back. No lecture. No pity. Just quiet presence and help. The kid breathes easier. Not because the burden is gone, but because they're no longer carrying it alone.

That child might be the younger you. And maybe today, someone still needs to tell you: it's okay to hand over part of the weight. Needing support doesn't make you a burden, it makes you beautifully, courageously human.

You were never meant to carry everything on your own. Let the love in.

Try This

Write a short letter to your younger self — the one dragging that oversized backpack. Tell them it's okay to ask for help. That they're not too much. That they don't have to be strong all the time. You can even begin with: *"Dear younger me, I saw how hard you were trying…"*

Then, choose one small burden you're carrying today — a worry, a to-do, an unspoken feeling — and share it with someone you trust. Text it, say it, or even write it down to bring up later. This is your reminder: letting someone carry a bit of the weight with you is an act of strength, not shame.

day 17: loved before you did anything

Scripture

"We love because he first loved us." — 1 John 4:19 (NIV)

Reflection

You didn't earn it.

You didn't prove yourself first.

You didn't have to show up, be strong, be good, be smart, be beautiful, or be perfect for God to love you.

That's the wild thing about grace. It interrupts the narrative of performance we grow up believing. From school grades to likes on a post, from parent approval to peer validation, it's always felt like you had to *do something* to be worthy. Be something. Achieve something. Impress someone.

But God's love doesn't work that way.

Before you had a resume, before you knew who you were, before you even knew how to pray — He chose you. Loved you. Said *you are mine*.

You might feel like you have to hustle to be worth something. But love like this? It's already given. No application. No audition. No qualifications needed.

Own Your Worth

Rest in that today: You are not a product of your performance. You are a recipient of grace. And nothing you do (or fail to do) can undo the love that found you first.

Journaling Questions

- Where in your life do you feel the need to *earn* love or approval?
- How does it feel to imagine being loved exactly as you are, with nothing to prove?
- What does "grace" mean to you right now?

Real Talk Quote

You didn't earn this love, and you can't lose it either.

Breath Prayer

Inhale: I am already loved.

Exhale: Before I did anything.

Need a soundtrack for today's reflection?

Scan to listen to "This Is Love" by King & Country.

Day 17: Loved Before You Did Anything

Creative Anchor

A worn-in sweater — the kind that knows your shape, fits just right, and doesn't ask you to change a thing. That's grace.

Try This

Wear something today that makes you feel fully *you*. There is no pressure to impress, just comfort. Let it be a reminder that you don't have to perform to be loved.

day 18: your pace has purpose

Scripture

"The Lord will work out his plans for my life—for your faithful love, O Lord, endures forever." — Psalm 138:8 (NLT)

Reflection

It's so easy to look around and feel like you're behind. Behind your friends. Behind the expectations. Behind where you thought you'd be by now. Social media doesn't help, it's a highlight reel of people "getting ahead," while you're wondering if you missed your cue.

But God doesn't rush good things. He works in seasons, not stopwatches. In fact, some of the most meaningful breakthroughs happen in the slow, quiet, ordinary moments when no one's watching. When you feel like nothing is happening, something sacred usually is.

Your story isn't running late. It's running deep.

This is your reminder: Your pace is not a mistake. It's protection. Preparation. Precision. You don't have to match someone else's timeline to be valid. What God is building in you requires a foundation that won't crack when the spotlight hits. The longer it takes, the more solid it will be.

Own Your Worth

Let yourself walk, not sprint. Let your life bloom in divine time, not a deadline.

Journaling Questions

- Where do you feel like you're "behind," and why?
- What gifts exist in this current pace or season?
- What would it mean to fully trust God's timeline for you?

Real Talk Quote

Your timing is not off, it's unfolding.

Breath Prayer

Inhale: I trust the pace.

Exhale: I let go of pressure.

Need a soundtrack for today's reflection?

Scan to listen to "Older" by Sasha Alex Sloan.

Day 18: Your Pace Has Purpose

Creative Anchor

A sundial — ancient, slow, and still accurate. Let this be your visual: steady, simple, and fully aligned with the light.

Try This

Write a letter to your future self one year from now. Describe what you hope she knows, feels, and has embraced by then.

day 19: your story isn't small

Scripture

"Though your beginning was small, your latter days will be very great."
— Job 8:7 (ESV)

Reflection

You might not have a million followers. You might not have a dramatic testimony. You might not be the loudest, boldest, or most accomplished person in the room. But hear this: Your story still matters. It is not small. It is sacred.

We live in a culture that glorifies big. Big platforms, big voices, big change. And while those things can be beautiful, they're not the only things that are valuable. God often works through the quiet, steady, unseen things. A conversation over coffee. A note sent in love. A moment of honesty that breaks someone's shame in half.

You don't need to sensationalize your life to make it meaningful. You just need to live it. The truth is, some of the most powerful stories are the ones that never get a spotlight. But they ripple. They heal. They matter.

If you've ever felt like your journey is too ordinary to matter, remember this: God chose shepherds to witness Jesus' birth. He used fishermen to build the Church. He gave a quiet girl named Mary the role of carrying the Savior of the world. There's no such thing as a small story in God's eyes, only stories that haven't been told yet.

So take heart. Live your story. Tell your truth. It's already more important than you think.

Journaling Questions

- In what ways have I downplayed the significance of my life or story?
- What small but meaningful moments have shaped me deeply?
- What part of my story do I feel afraid to tell and why?

Real Talk Quote

Your story doesn't need to be loud to be powerful.

Breath Prayer

Inhale: My life has meaning.

Exhale: My story matters.

Need a soundtrack for today's reflection?

Scan to listen to "Storyteller" by Morgan Harper Nichols.

Day 19: Your Story Isn't Small

Creative Anchor

"There is no greater agony than bearing an untold story inside you." — Maya Angelou

Let this remind you: even the quietest life holds volumes. What you've lived through, felt, learned, lost, and loved. It matters.

Try This

Choose one part of your story, even a small scene, and write it out as if you were telling it to a friend. No edits, no disclaimers. Let it breathe.

day 20: you are not too late

Scripture

"The Lord is not slow in keeping his promise, as some understand slowness. Instead, he is patient with you..." — 2 Peter 3:9 (NIV)

Reflection

You know that panicked feeling when you feel behind in life. Maybe your friends are hitting milestones — degrees, marriages, babies, businesses — and you're still figuring out how to get out of bed without a battle. It can make you feel like you missed something. Like you've somehow fallen out of sync with your own life.

But here's what's real: you're not too late. There is no timeline you were supposed to follow like a script. Life is not a race, and your worth isn't measured by your pace.

God doesn't rush healing. He doesn't panic over your timeline. He is not anxious about your "delays." He's doing a deeper work and sometimes, the most sacred things take the longest. Redemption takes time. Becoming takes time. Growth beneath the surface isn't visible, but it's still happening.

You're not behind. You're not broken. You're just becoming. And God hasn't forgotten you. He's not disappointed. He's not waiting at the finish line, tapping His foot. He's walking *with* you, step by shaky step, teaching you to trust Him over your own schedule.

Own Your Worth

You may be waiting, wandering, or just plain weary, but none of it is wasted. You are right where you need to be. God is still writing. You're not late to your life. You're on time for your healing.

Journaling Questions

- Where do I feel behind or like I've missed my chance?
- How might God be working *in* the delay, not despite it?
- What would it look like to trust divine timing today?

Real Talk Quote

You're not too late. Some of the best things bloom in their own time.

Breath Prayer

Inhale: I release the rush.

Exhale: I receive divine timing.

Need a soundtrack for today's reflection?

Scan to listen to *"Bloom" by The Paper Kites.*

This gentle, indie favorite is a musical exhale — tender, patient, and full of quiet beauty. It echoes the truth that growth doesn't have to be rushed.

Day 20: You Are Not Too Late

Creative Anchor

An hourglass — a reminder that divine timing can't be hurried or delayed.

Try This

Take a deep breath and set a timer for 10 minutes. In that quiet, write a letter to your future self who no longer feels behind. What does she know now?

day 21: you don't need to earn love

Scripture

"But God demonstrates his own love for us in this: While we were still sinners, Christ died for us." — Romans 5:8 (NIV)

Reflection

A lot of us walk around thinking love has to be earned. We'll be enough once we're successful, kind enough, attractive enough, and low-maintenance enough. We'll be loved once we've stopped messing up, doubting, and needing.

But that's not how real love works and definitely not how God's love works.

Romans 5:8 says something wild: *"While we were still sinners…"* Not after we got our act together. Not when we finally started healing. Not when we made ourselves easier to love. While we were still messy, confused, hurting, and trying, Christ loved us enough to die for us. That's the blueprint of grace.

You don't have to perform for love. You don't have to earn your way into God's presence. You already have His love, not because you proved yourself, but because He chose you. That kind of love is healing. It's freeing. It says: *You don't have to be perfect to be held.*

Own Your Worth

What would it look like if you stopped trying to *deserve* love and started simply *receiving* it?

You are not a transaction. You are a beloved human being. And the sooner you stop chasing conditional love, the sooner you'll experience the radical peace of unconditional belonging.

Journaling Questions

- Where in your life have you felt like love had to be earned?
- What would it mean to believe you're already fully loved, without fixing, proving, or hustling?
- How can you practice receiving love without guilt or apology?

Real Talk Quote

You don't have to hustle for what God already gave you for free.

Breath Prayer

Inhale: I am already loved.

Exhale: I don't need to earn it.

Day 21: You Don't Need to Earn Love

Need a soundtrack for today's reflection?

Scan to listen to "Who You Are" by Jessie J.

This track is a soft but powerful reminder that even when you don't feel lovable, you are, deeply and completely.

Creative Anchor

Visualize a handwritten letter addressed to *you*, not from a person but God. What would it say? What would He remind you of? Imagine the envelope reading: "To the one I've always loved." Maybe write it out today.

Try This

Look in the mirror today and say out loud, "I don't have to earn love. I already have it." Say it twice. Say it until it doesn't feel awkward anymore.

day 22: your voice matters

Scripture

"Do not say, 'I am too young.' You must go to everyone I send you to and say whatever I command you. Do not be afraid of them, for I am with you and will rescue you," declares the Lord. — Jeremiah 1:7–8 (NIV)

Reflection

You've probably been told to stay quiet directly or indirectly. Maybe someone rolled their eyes when you spoke up. Maybe you were shut down, corrected, laughed at, or simply ignored. Over time, that does something to you. It makes you question if your words carry weight, if your opinions matter, if your voice deserves a place at the table.

But here's what's real: God gave you your voice, your personality, your thoughts, your style of communicating for a reason. And the world needs it.

Your voice doesn't have to be the loudest to be powerful. You don't need to dominate a room to speak the truth. Whether you write, whisper, sing, speak, or create, your voice can shift atmospheres, comfort others, spark ideas, or start healing.

Jeremiah thought he was too young, too unqualified, too small to be a messenger. But God didn't see lack — He saw purpose. And He reminded Jeremiah that He'd be with him. Always.

Own Your Worth

You don't need a massive platform or perfect delivery. You just need courage to speak what matters with love, with truth, and with the deep knowing that your words matter because **you** matter.

So use your voice today, not to impress, not to perform, but to show up, tell the truth, and light the path for someone else who's still finding theirs.

Journaling Questions

• When have you felt like your voice didn't matter? What happened?

• What's something you've wanted to say but held back?

• What would change if you believed your words carried weight?

Real Talk Quote

Your voice doesn't have to be loud to be powerful.

Breath Prayer

Inhale: My voice matters.

Exhale: I will speak with courage.

Need a soundtrack for today's reflection?

Scan to listen to "Speak Life" by TobyMac.

Day 22: Your Voice Matters

Creative Anchor

A lit match in a dark room — small, quiet, and yet it changes everything. Your words can do the same.

Try This

Record yourself speaking a truth you need to believe. Play it back. Let it sink in. Speak it again tomorrow a bit louder.

day 23: trust the unfolding

Scripture

"Being confident of this, that he who began a good work in you will carry it on to completion until the day of Christ Jesus." — Philippians 1:6 (NIV)

Reflection

Some days you want to fast-forward. You want to skip the uncertainty, the waiting, the messy middle. You want the answers, the healing, the happy ending now.

But life doesn't hand out spoilers. It unfolds slowly. And that's hard when you're wired to chase outcomes and checkboxes.

Here's what's true, even in the fog: God is not done with you.

You may feel like you're in the in-between — not who you were, not yet who you want to be. But even now, something holy is forming. Growth doesn't always announce itself with fireworks. Sometimes it's quiet. Invisible. A becoming you can't yet see.

Your story doesn't need to be polished to be purposeful. God isn't waiting for you to "arrive" before He works. He's in the middle of your mess, your questions, your slow progress.

You don't need to have everything figured out to be held by grace. Just keep showing up. Keep listening. Keep trusting the unfolding.

Own Your Worth

Journaling Questions

- What part of your life feels unfinished or unclear right now?
- How does this verse help you reframe your process?
- What would it look like to trust God's work in progress, including you?

Real Talk Quote

God's not finished, and neither are you.

Breath Prayer

Inhale: You began this good work.

Exhale: I trust you to finish it.

Need a soundtrack for today's reflection?

Scan to listen to "Canvas and Clay" by Pat Barrett.

Day 23: Trust the Unfolding

Creative Anchor

An embroidery hoop — from the back, it looks like a mess of knots and tangles. But flip it over? It's a work of art in progress.

Try This

Do something today that's unfinished — write one paragraph, take one small step, tidy one corner. Celebrate the progress, not perfection.

day 24: live from your worth

Scripture

"In repentance and rest is your salvation, in quietness and trust is your strength." — Isaiah 30:15 (NIV)

Reflection

You don't have to hustle to matter. You don't have to shout to be heard. You don't need to prove your value through performance, perfection, or productivity. Your worth isn't earned, it's inherent. It was spoken over you long before the world ever tried to measure you.

Still, it's hard not to internalize the pressure. Maybe you were praised for being an overachiever. The reliable one. The one who always said yes. So now, when you rest, you feel guilty. When you say no, you feel selfish. When you're quiet, you wonder if you're fading.

But Scripture flips that upside down. It doesn't say your strength is in striving. It says your strength is in **quietness** and **trust**. It's in the pause. The no. The deep breath. The sacred space where you remember: *You are already enough.*

Living from your worth means moving through the world with an inner stillness that doesn't need constant applause. It means being

Own Your Worth

grounded in who you are, not who you're trying to impress. It's not arrogance, it's anchored confidence.

Let that sink in. You're allowed to live like your value isn't up for negotiation. You're allowed to rest. To step back. To choose slow. That doesn't make you less. It reveals how much you've already grown.

You don't have to prove a thing. You get to live from the truth that it's already been proven: You're beloved.

Journaling Questions

- Where in your life do you feel the pressure to prove your worth?
- What does "quiet strength" look like to you?
- What would change if you really believed your value wasn't up for debate?

Real Talk Quote

You don't have to chase what's already yours.

Breath Prayer

Inhale: My worth is settled

Exhale: I live from it, not for it

Day 24: Live from Your Worth

Need a soundtrack for today's reflection?

Scan to listen to "More Than Enough" by Sarah Reeves.

Creative Anchor

A river stone—smooth, weathered, and solid. It doesn't shout, but it holds its ground.

Try This

Take a few minutes today to rest without your phone or to-do list. Just breathe. Just be. Let it remind you: doing less doesn't make you less.

day 25: you're allowed to be a work in progress

Scripture

"For I am the Lord your God who takes hold of your right hand and says to you, Do not fear; I will help you." — Isaiah 41:13 (NIV)

Reflection

Sometimes you feel like you should be further along. Like healing should be quicker. Growth should be tidier. Faith should be stronger. But the truth is, becoming takes time.

You are not behind. You are not broken. You are becoming.

There's no finish line you need to sprint to. No invisible deadline to hit. You're allowed to have questions, doubts, slow days, and setbacks. God doesn't measure your progress by perfection—He measures it by presence.

Even when you're unraveling, you are still held. Even in the pause, grace is working. Even when you don't feel worthy, you are still wildly loved.

Let go of the pressure to be "done." You're not late. You're alive. And that's enough.

Own Your Worth

Journaling Questions
- Where are you holding yourself to unrealistic expectations?
- What would change if you gave yourself more grace?
- How can you recognize progress even when it feels small?

Real Talk Quote

Progress isn't linear, and neither is healing.

Breath Prayer

Inhale: I'm a work in progress

Exhale: And that's okay

Need a soundtrack for today's reflection?

Scan to listen to "Slow Down" by Nichole Nordeman.

Day 25: You're Allowed to Be a Work in Progress

Creative Anchor

A patchwork quilt stitched slowly, piece by piece. Beautiful not because it's perfect, but because it's made with care.

Try This

Write a kind note to your younger self, and read it aloud. Then write one to your current self. Speak to yourself like someone who's becoming, not someone who's failing.

day 26: you were never too much

Scripture

"You are altogether beautiful, my darling; there is no flaw in you." — Song of Solomon 4:7 (NIV)

Reflection

Maybe you've been told out loud or through sideways glances that you feel too deeply, speak too boldly, dream too big. Perhaps someone's labeled your passion as drama, your honesty as trouble, your energy as chaos. And maybe you started editing yourself. Shrinking in public. Apologizing before you even spoke. Holding back joy because it felt like "too much."

But what if all of that intensity wasn't a liability, but a light?

God didn't design you to be palatable. He didn't call you to be agreeable, silent, or "easy to manage." He made you with spark and spirit, with dimensions and contradictions, with a voice that matters and a presence that carries weight. The fullness of who you are — yes, even the bold, sensitive, curious parts — is not an error to correct. It's a gift to honor.

You don't have to tone down your personality to be accepted. You don't have to dilute your truth to fit in. You weren't made for invisibility. You were made to show up, stand tall, and take up the space love carved out for you.

Own Your Worth

Being "a lot" isn't a flaw. It's a kind of beauty that refuses to go unnoticed. The people who truly see you will never ask you to be less. They'll thank you for being exactly as you are.

So let today be the day you stop asking for permission to be whole.

Journaling Questions

• What parts of you have you quieted or questioned in order to feel more "acceptable"?

• Who told you you were too much, and why might they have been wrong?

• What would it feel like to live unapologetically in your full expression?

Real Talk Quote

You're not too much. You're a whole story and you're still being written.

Breath Prayer

Inhale: I am not too much

Exhale: I am beautifully made

Need a soundtrack for today's reflection?

Scan to listen to "In My Blood" by Shawn Mendes.

Day 26: You Were Never Too Much

Creative Anchor

A wildflower, untamed, vibrant, unapologetically alive. It grows where it wants to, not where it's told to.

Try This

Make a list of five things you've been told were "too much" about you and beside each one, write why it's actually a gift.

day 27: stay soft

Scripture

"I will give you a new heart and put a new spirit in you; I will remove from you your heart of stone and give you a heart of flesh." — Ezekiel 36:26 (NIV)

Reflection

You've been told to toughen up. Harden. Build walls.

And maybe you did. Because life? It stings. People leave. Words cut. Trust gets broken. So you protected yourself. You stopped letting things in, even the good.

But that kind of safety comes at a cost. When we numb pain, we often numb joy, too.

You weren't created to live behind armor. You were made with a heart that feels. Those hopes. That breaks and heals and loves again.

Softness is not weakness. It takes **courage** to stay open in a world that's taught you to close off. It's powerful to feel deeply, to cry when it hurts, to celebrate out loud, to still believe in goodness even when it's rare.

God doesn't shame your tenderness. He created it. He gives you a new heart, not one hardened by survival, but one softened by grace.

Let this be your rebellion: stay soft.

Let it be your strength: you still care.

And let it be your truth: you are never too much for the right kind of love.

Journaling Questions

- Where have you felt the need to harden your heart to protect yourself?
- What would staying soft look like in one part of your life this week?
- How has God shown you that tenderness is strength?

Real Talk Quote

It's brave to feel deeply in a world that tells you to go numb.

Breath Prayer

Inhale: Give me a soft heart.

Exhale: Let me feel and still heal.

Day 27: Stay Soft

Need a soundtrack for today's reflection?

Scan to listen to "Only" by RY X.

Creative Anchor

A paper boat on water — delicate, but afloat. It moves forward, not because it's indestructible, but because it's brave.

Try This

Write a letter to your younger self. Let the words be soft, kind, and full of grace. Then read it aloud to remind yourself of how far you've come.

day 28: you are allowed to take up joy

Scripture

"You make known to me the path of life; in your presence there is fullness of joy." — Psalm 16:11 (ESV)

Reflection

Joy doesn't have to be justified.

You don't need a clean house, a fixed past, or a perfect plan to laugh out loud or let yourself smile until your cheeks hurt. You don't need to wait for everything to settle before you let the light in. Joy is not a reward for finally getting it right. It's a lifeline for walking through the mess.

But many of us learned to treat joy like a luxury. Something to be earned after the work is done, after the healing is finished, after the crisis has passed. As if joy only belongs on the mountaintop, not in the in-between. As if it's irresponsible to feel lightness when life feels heavy.

But here's the radical truth: joy is not an afterthought. It's part of the medicine.

It doesn't mean you're ignoring pain — it means you're letting light in anyway. And sometimes, that's the bravest thing you can do.

God delights in your delight. Yes, even yours. The quiet grin when you hear your favorite song. The way your shoulders drop when you step into the sunshine. The weird little thing that makes you laugh until your sides ache. He doesn't just tolerate your joy — He joins you in it.

You don't need to shrink your joy to make others comfortable. You don't need to feel bad for feeling good. Let joy rise in the cracks. Let it sit beside your grief. Let it remind you that healing isn't only about surviving, it's also about living.

Journaling Questions

• What does joy look or feel like to you right now?

• Do you ever feel guilty about enjoying your life? Where might that come from?

• What's one small way you can welcome joy today?

Real Talk Quote

Joy isn't a reward, it's a rebellion against despair.

Breath Prayer

Inhale: I choose joy, even now.

Exhale: It's safe to feel it.

Day 28: You Are Allowed to Take Up Joy

Need a soundtrack for today's reflection?

Scan to listen to "Good Day" by Surfaces.

Creative Anchor

A sunbeam breaking through a cloudy sky — joy doesn't erase the clouds, but it reminds you the light is still there.

Try This

Do something small today that sparks joy even if no one else gets it. Watch your favorite meme, wear your favorite outfit, or eat your favorite snack with zero apology.

day 29: you're more than your low moments

Scripture

"The Lord is close to the brokenhearted and saves those who are crushed in spirit." — Psalm 34:18 (NIV)

Reflection

You know those days when everything feels heavy?

When your heart aches for reasons you can't quite name? When the world keeps spinning, but you feel stuck? On those days, even getting out of bed is a quiet act of courage. Even brushing your teeth or replying to a text is a win. And yet, those moments can feel like failure — like you're falling behind, like you should be stronger by now.

But here's the truth:

Low moments don't define you. They don't disqualify you from love or discredit your worth. They don't cancel out the good that lives inside you.

You are not your struggle.

You are not your burnout or your breakdown.

You are not the voice that says, "You're too broken to be loved."

God doesn't back away when you're struggling.

Own Your Worth

He comes closer. He draws near, not because you've earned it, but because He loves you especially in the places that feel raw and undone. When the light dims and hope feels far, He doesn't wait for you to climb your way back up. He meets you on the floor. Right where you are.

Being human means having hard days. But being held by grace means you don't have to go through them alone.

You are still whole in the waiting. Still worthy of the weeping. Still loved in the quiet ache.

So let today be gentle. Let your breath be enough. Let the fact that you're still here be your proof of strength.

You are not just surviving, you are learning, healing, unfolding. And none of this is wasted.

You are more than your low moments. You are still becoming.

Journaling Questions

• What thoughts do you tend to believe about yourself on hard days?

• How might God's nearness shift how you experience your low moments?

• What would grace look like today, from yourself, for yourself?

Real Talk Quote

You are not the worst thing that's ever happened to you.

Breath Prayer

Inhale: Even now, you are near.

Exhale: Even here, I am loved.

Day 29: You're More Than Your Low Moments

Need a soundtrack for today's reflection?

Scan to listen to "Call It Grace" by Unspoken.

Creative Anchor

You were never just "enough" —

You were made to light the sky.

Not by striving, not by proving,

Just by standing tall and trying.

Try This

Write a note to your future self for the next time you're in a low place. Let your words be soft, real, and kind. Seal it somewhere special.

day 30: the work was worth it

Scripture

"And after you have suffered a little while, the God of all grace... will himself restore, confirm, strengthen, and establish you." — 1 Peter 5:10 (ESV)

Reflection

You've come a long way.

Not just through thirty days of reading and reflecting but through the deep, soul-stretching work of returning to yourself.

You showed up.

On days you didn't feel like it. On days the lies felt louder than truth. On days you weren't sure, this would make a difference. But still, you came.

You dared to pause. To listen. To name what hurt. To believe that healing was possible.

And maybe no one else noticed.

Maybe there were no gold stars or applause. But the work you did here? It was holy.

You untangled shame.

Own Your Worth

You questioned the stories that kept you small.

You stopped apologizing for being who you are.

You remembered what the world made you forget — that you are already loved.

And no, this journey hasn't tied up into a neat little bow. But that was never the goal.

You were never meant to become a shinier version of yourself.

You were meant to *come home* to yourself.

This is not the end. It's the turning point. A marker in the dirt that says: *I went deeper here. I found truth here. I grew here.*

You are stronger now, not because the road was easy, but because you stayed on it.

You are softer now, not because you gave up, but because you let grace in.

You are still becoming and that is more than enough.

So celebrate. You didn't just finish something. You *transformed* something.

The work was worth it.

And so are you.

Journaling Questions

• What has shifted in you since Day 1?

• What belief do you now hold that you didn't before?

• What would you say to your past self — the one who almost didn't start?

Real Talk Quote

You didn't just read this book, you *showed up for yourself*. That's power.

Breath Prayer

Inhale: I am not who I was.

Day 30: The Work Was Worth It

Exhale: And I am still becoming.

Need a soundtrack for today's reflection?

Scan to listen to "The Middle" by Zedd, Maren Morris, Grey.

Creative Anchor

A tree ring — quiet proof that growth happened, even when no one was watching. Each layer tells a story. Each line says, I made it through another year. That's you now. Steady. Rooted. Becoming.

Try This

Celebrate your journey. Light a candle. Write a letter to your future self. Take a quiet walk and breathe in what you've just done. Or simply whisper: "I did that."

You've earned this. Keep becoming.

conclusion: keep showing up

You made it.

Not just to the last page of this book, but through thirty days of showing up for your story, your heart, your healing. That's no small thing. In a world that keeps telling you to shrink, stay quiet, or be someone else, you chose to slow down and listen for the truth instead.

You've walked through some hard territory: the lies that said you weren't enough, the shame that whispered you should be different, the doubt that made you question if any of this really mattered. And yet, here you are. Still becoming. Still rising. Still here.

That's strength.

You've done the sacred work of remembering that your value isn't something you earn. It's something you carry. It's stitched into you by the One who made you, long before anyone had the chance to tell you otherwise.

But this journey doesn't end here. The loudness of life — the distractions, the pressure, the outside opinions — will still come. What changes now is how you meet them.

You've reclaimed your worth. Now it's time to protect it.

Conclusion: Keep Showing Up

In *Protect Your Peace*, the third book in the *Anchored* series, we'll step into the next chapter together, learning how to hold on to what's true, quiet the noise, and live from a place that's rooted, not rattled.

You're ready. I believe that with my whole heart.

So take a breath. Let it land.

And carry this with you: You are not a question mark. You are a declaration.

With love,

Emery Knox

before you go...

If this devotional reminded you of your worth,
would you consider leaving a quick review?
Just a few honest words can help someone else
who's searching for something real and encouraging.
Thanks for being here.

Thanks for showing up.

With love,
 — **Emery**

www.ingramcontent.com/pod-product-compliance
Lightning Source LLC
Chambersburg PA
CBHW060455080526
44584CB00015B/1440